Foggy

By Juniata Rogers

Would you like to walk through clouds? You can. Just go outside on a foggy day. Fog is a cloud on the ground.

Fog can make it hard to see things in the distance.

Water vapor is forming over this pond.

Fog forms because of **water vapor** in the air. Water vapor is water that is a **gas**. Air is also a gas. It doesn't have a shape. It spreads out as much as it can.

Warm air can hold more vapor than cold air. When air cools, the vapor **condenses**—it forms tiny water droplets. These droplets float in the air to make fog.

Most of this forest has been covered by fog.

Lights are helpful in this foggy park.

Fog usually forms at night. At night, the land cools the warm air above it. But fog can form in daytime if warm air blows into a cold spot.

Mountains are often foggy. The air on a mountain is cool and wet. During the day, warm air flows up the mountain. It meets the cool air, and fog forms.

These mountains in China are covered in fog.

Fog on the ocean is called sea smoke.

Fog also forms over water. Air above water holds a lot of water vapor. Wind over the water doesn't need to cool it much to make fog.

In winter, fog makes the world slippery. **Freezing fog** contains frozen droplets. It leaves ice wherever it goes.

Freezing fog has put frost on this tree's branches.

Ice fog floats over the St. Lawrence River near Montreal.

Ice fog holds bits of ice the size of dust. It only forms in very cold weather. Parts of Alaska and Canada experience ice fog.

Foggy days are dangerous. Fog is hard to see through. Drivers might need to pull over. Pilots might cancel flights.

Drivers must use their headlights on foggy days.

Foggy days can be very peaceful.

Foggy days can be magical, too. Trees can look like shadows. The air is cool and wet. Water gathers on the grass. What will you do on your next foggy day?

Glossary

condense (kun-DENSS): To turn from gas to water.

freezing fog (FREE-zing FAWG): Fog that holds water that is colder than ice. When it touches something colder than 32 degrees Fahrenheit, it freezes instantly.

gas (GAS) Gas is what liquids become when they are heated. Gas doesn't hold a shape. It tends to spread out as much as it can.

ice fog (EYCE FAWG): Fog that forms when it's extremely cold. Instead of water, ice fog is made from floating bits of ice.

water vapor (WAH-tur VAY-pur): Water in the form of a gas.

To Find Out More

Books

De Steve, Karen. *Little Kids First Big Book of Weather.* Washington, DC: National Geographic Children's Books, 2017.

Kudlinski, Kathleen V. *Boy, Were We Wrong About the Weather.* New York, NY: Dial Books, 2015.

Rattini, Kristin Baird. *National Geographic Readers: Weather.* Washington, DC: National Geographic Children's Books, 2013.

Websites

Visit our website for links about fog:
childsworld.com/links

Note to Parents, Teachers, and Librarians: We routinely verify our Web links to make sure they are safe and active sites. So encourage your readers to check them out!

Index

About the Author

Juniata Rogers grew up in Newport, Rhode Island. She has worked as a naturalist, an art model, and a teacher. She's been writing professionally for 25 years, and currently lives near Washington, DC.

The Child's World®
childsworld.com

Published by The Child's World®
1980 Lookout Drive • Mankato, MN 56003-1705
800-599-READ • www.childsworld.com

Photo credits: Doidam 10/Shutterstock.com: 4; Ivan Kurmyshov/Shutterstock.com: 12; Jaromir Chalabala/Shutterstock.com: 20; Marc Bruxelle/Shutterstock.com: 16; Montypeter/Shutterstock.com: 19; Nickolay Khoroshkov/Shutterstock.com: 7; Nicola Bertolini/Shutterstock.com: 8; Regina Sarkuviene/Shutterstock.com: 15; Robsonphoto/Shutterstock.com: 3; Roxana Bashyrova/Shutterstock.com: cover, 1; wabbit photo/Shutterstock.com: 11

ISBN Hardcover: 9781503827875
ISBN Paperback: 9781622434558
LCCN: 2018939779

Printed in the United States of America • PA02398